THE TABLETOP LEARNING SERIES

SCIENCE FUN

Discovering the World Around You

by Imogene Forte

Incentive Publications, Inc.
Nashville, Tennessee

Illustrated by Gayle Seaberg Harvey
Cover designed by Mary Hamilton and illustrated by Jan Cunningham
Edited by Susan Oglander

Library of Congress Catalog Number 84-62935
ISBN 0-86530-100-X

THIS
SCIENCE FUN BOOK
BELONGS TO

_____

CONTENTS

EXPERIMENTING

GO FOR THE FACTS

The questioning, investigating, exploring and experimenting scientists do is what sets them apart from other people. If you want to begin to think and act like a real scientist, you need to start posing your own questions and trying to find better and more scientific answers to them.

Print each of your questions on a 5" x 7" index card and keep the cards in a readily available box. Then, begin to think about the best way to find the answers or to solve the problems. Will you need to look the answer up in a book, consult an authority for help, go on an expedition or do an experiment?

All the projects in **Science Fun** will help you find out about the topic in one way. Some are investigations, some explorations and some experiments. You won't need a lot of expensive supplies because most of the projects use common things you already have around the house or classroom. You may even think of your own ways to arrive at other scientific facts and conclusions. Try to be creative and use as many resources as possible to help you.

As you find answers to your questions, write them on the back of the cards. Give a very brief account of how you found the answer, date it and return the card to the box. You will now have a permanent record of your scientific activity. You can use your box to make up games, to help you with your homework or for science fair projects. More importantly, you will be learning and growing and becoming better at thinking and acting in a truly scientific manner.

Imogene Forte

INVESTIGATING

MY OWN INVESTIGATIONS

TRICKY TRIVIA

Here are a few "tricky" science questions to strain your brain and get you started on the road to thinking like a true scientist.

You will find some of them used in the projects in **Science Fun**; others you will have to figure out on your own.

You could make up a science trivia game, a concentration or lotto game or even a board game using the questions.

However you decide to use them, keep adding to the list until you have at least thirty. Just doing that should make you smarter!

1. Which came first, the chicken or the egg?
2. How do birds know when it is time to fly south each winter?
3. How do tadpoles turn into frogs?
4. What really happened to all the dinosaurs?
5. Which came first, the acorn or the oak?
6. Who discovered gravity, how and when?
7. What causes hiccups?
8. Why can't animals talk?
9. What causes thunder and lightning?
10. Why is the ocean salty?
11. What causes viruses?
12. How do glaciers form?
13. What causes freckles?

MACHINES AT WORK

People usually think of machines as large, complicated devices with lots of movable parts. The scientific view of a machine however, is any device that is used to transform or transfer energy. Scientists think of machines as valuable objects that make a task easier to accomplish. A tiny pocket screwdriver is classified as a machine just as is a huge trailer truck.

The energy to activate machines comes from sources such as electricity, gasoline, wind, water and muscles.

To help you become more knowledgeable about the machines around you and to sharpen your scientific awareness, try to spend a couple of hours exploring *every* machine you encounter. Try to determine the use of the machine and its source of power.

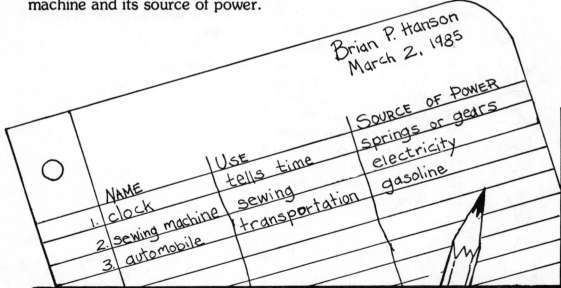

Brian P. Hanson
March 2, 1985

NAME	Use	Source of Power
1. clock	tells time	springs or gears
2. sewing machine	sewing	electricity
3. automobile	transportation	gasoline

WORK-WISE MACHINES

To demonstrate how ordinary, taken-for-granted machines make daily life easier, try accomplishing these tasks as you would have to in a machineless world.

Divide a piece of cloth into three equal strips by tearing it with your hands. Now, try using scissors. Try cracking a nut without a nutcracker. Then, try it with a nutcracker. Try opening a can without a can opener. Then, try it with a can opener. Try sharpening a pencil without a pencil sharpener. Then, try it with a pencil sharpener. Aren't you glad we have machines around to help?

BODY WORKS

So, you never thought of your body as a machine. Well, it is! As a matter of fact, the human body is the most marvelous machine of all. Just like other machines, your body needs fuel to power it; it needs to be kept clean; all of its parts need adjusting and "fixing" when necessary; and its parts need constant use.

For this activity you will need a piece of butcher paper large enough to draw your body shape on. You will also need a pencil, scissors, a felt tip pen and resource books.

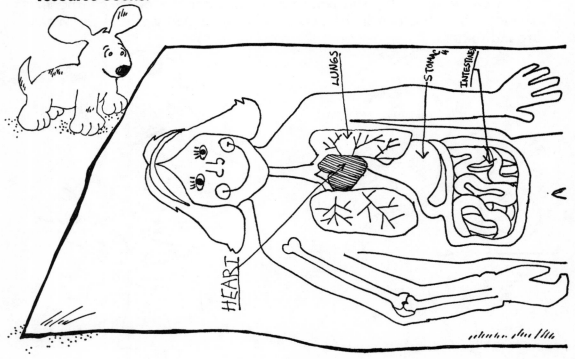

Tack the paper to the wall or stretch it out on the floor. Either stand against the paper on the wall, or stretch out on it on the floor.

Place your arms at your sides. Ask someone to trace your body shape onto the paper with a pencil. Be sure to trace your hands and feet. Draw around the traced shape with the felt tip pen. Cut the shape out. Use the pen to draw hair and facial features on the traced shape.

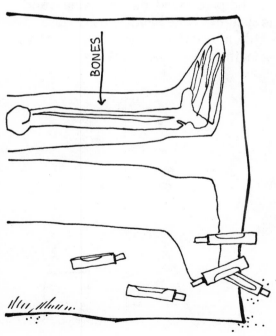

Now, the fun begins.

Locate and draw in as many body parts as you possibly can (with the help of resource books).

Label the parts and find out what each one does. The more parts you can draw and label, the better.

Did you ever dream that your body was such a marvelous machine?

17

WHAT'S IN IT FOR ME?

Would you eat a big spoonful of pyridoxine hydrochloride? Take a dose of beta carotene or swallow ten drops of zinc or copper? Or, wash your mouth out with sodium monofluorophosphate? Chances are, if you have ever eaten packaged cereal, canned soup or taken vitamins, you have put at least one or more of these substances in your body. Do you really know what is in the foods you eat?

Gather some items from the bathroom and kitchen and grab a pencil and paper. Look at the labels on toothpaste, cough syrup, cereal, canned vegetables, etc. Jot down some common ingredients or those you might have questions about. Look up the words to help explain what effects these items have on the human body. Some help to build strong bones and muscles, some are good for the nervous system, some have no use at all and some can even be harmful. After this little investigation, you will be more aware of "what's in it for you" when selecting food and drink.

18

A BANQUET FOR THE BIRDS

Roll one cup of peanut butter around in a package of birdseed (or sunflower seeds if you have them) until a ball is formed. Squeeze the ball with your hands until it holds together good and tight. Place the birds' banquet on a windowsill or a fence post on a cold day. The cold air will harden the ball and the grateful birds will flock to it. Keep a record of the birds that take advantage of your hospitality and try to learn as much as you can about each kind. Be sure to keep feeding them — they will rely on you for their winter food.

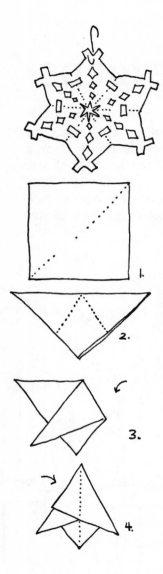

LET IT SNOW, LET IT SNOW

Look at some snowflakes under a magnifying glass. Did you know that no two snowflakes are exactly alike even though they all have six sides? Observe the snow falling. Then, feel, taste and experiment with some snowflakes while the snow is still fresh and new. If you don't live in an area where it snows, cut six-sided snowflakes from white paper. Even if you do have snow, these snowflakes are fun to make. With a twisted paper clip for a hanger, they also make great Christmas tree or window decorations.

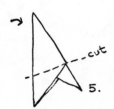

5.

cut

cut out any shapes

6.

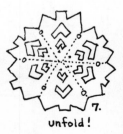

unfold!

7.

MORE ABOUT SNOW

Here's an experiment for those who have access to all that white wintery stuff. Collect some snow in a bowl. Divide the snow into three small bowls. Now, place one bowl in the refrigerator, one in the freezer and leave one on a table. Check the three bowls in about 30 minutes to see what has happened. What causes snow? Is it clean enough to eat? Is it heavier before or after it melts?

A PERISCOPIC VIEW OF THE WORLD

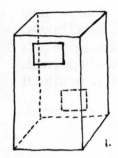

Scientists have devised many instruments that enable people to take a different look at the world in which they live. Among these instruments are the telescope, microscope, binoculars, hand lens, kaleidoscope, camera and periscope.

You can make your own periscope and look at the world around you in a whole new way.

You will need:
- a narrow box (shoe box)
- two mirrors (small sturdy ones)
- glue
- masking tape
- scissors
- poster paints

1. Cut two rectangular windows from the long sides of the box at opposite ends (see illustration).
2. Glue or tape mirrors inside the box across from each window. You will need to adjust one of the mirrors to make the periscope work. First, glue the top mirror. Then, look through the bottom window and carefully move the bottom mirror until it catches the reflection from the top mirror and you can see out the top window. Glue the bottom mirror in place.
3. Put the lid on the box and seal it with masking tape.
4. Paint a nice design on your periscope and start looking around!

RAIN, RAIN IS ON THE WAY

Can you find out why before a rainstorm ...

... people with curly hair find their hair curlier, and people with straight hair find their hair limp?

... animals become nervous and restless?

- cats may meow and clean themselves more
- pigs wallow about and squeal
- cows huddle together as if seeking comfort from each other
- horses "switch and twitch" and sometimes bolt
- insects fly low and bite more
- birds chirp more loudly

... some plants close their blossoms, fold up or turn over their leaves?

- dandelions close their blossoms tightly

- morning glories "tuck in" their blooms as if ready for a long nap

- clover folds up its leaves

- leaves on many trees roll up or show their undersides

... older people and people with joint or muscle problems such as rheumatism or arthritis have stiffness and discomfort?

Ask an older person to give you some more sure signs of "rain on the way." Then use a reference book to find out why these signs would appear.

HOW DO YOU MEASURE UP?

Look around your home or classroom for all the items you can find that are used for measuring. Make a graph similar to the one below to show what the different items are used to measure.

How many of these items do you use every day?
Which one do you use most often?
Which one is the most expensive?

TIME FLIES

And while you are on the subject of measuring, why not make a "Time Flies" collage for your wall. You will need:

- some old magazines and mail-order catalogs
- scissors
- paste
- felt tip pen
- heavy construction paper or cardboard

Cut out pictures of all different kinds of things that are used to measure time. Look for watches, clocks and sundials. Arrange them attractively on the construction paper or cardboard. Then, paste the pictures in place. Leave room to print the title of your collage before hanging it on the wall to enjoy.

ONCE UPON A COLOR

Can you imagine how drab and uninteresting the world would be if everything were the same color?

Just for fun, try to imagine what your world would be like if all the animals, plants and minerals were red. You would have red bears, red lettuce, a red sky and even red rocks! Wouldn't it be strange to see only people with red hair, red eyes and red skin? Red apples, red birds and red roses are beautiful, but how would you like bright red dogs, red milk and red trees?

Pick your favorite color and imagine a world in which everything is that color. After you have thought about it for awhile, try to think of the color you would choose if you had to live in a one-color world. Think about why you chose that color.

Now, take a sheet of paper and a box of crayons. Go outside and find a place to sit quietly for five minutes. Start a scribble drawing with a crayon from your box each time you spot an item of that color. When five minutes are up, your scribble drawing will give you a new look at the "colors in your world."

SHOE BOX TAKE-IT-APART KIT

Have you ever found that preparing for a special time is almost as much fun as actually experiencing the event? Since this activity requires some advanced planning, you should get started today!

First, you will need a shoe box. If you are more adventurous, you might need a large boot box to house your kit. Then the hunt is on for discarded or broken clocks, calculators, radios, cameras, fishing reels or any other mechanical object that is no longer used by its owner. Remove any electrical plugs or wires from larger appliances before adding them to your kit. (Ask a grownup for help if you are not sure how to do this.) You will also need as many small tools as you can collect — screwdrivers, tack hammers and tweezers. Now you are ready for that day when you are just a little bit bored and need something interesting to do.

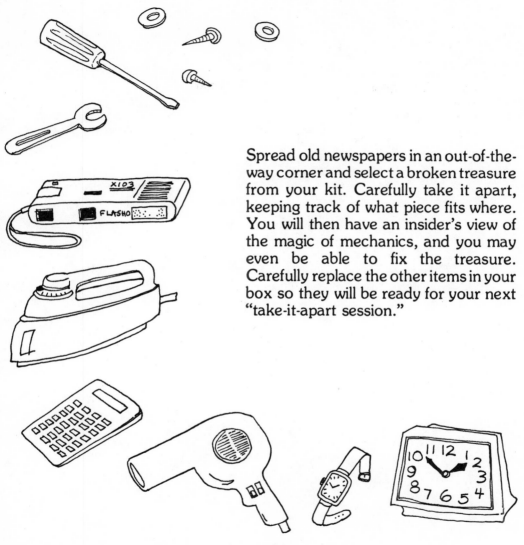

Spread old newspapers in an out-of-the-way corner and select a broken treasure from your kit. Carefully take it apart, keeping track of what piece fits where. You will then have an insider's view of the magic of mechanics, and you may even be able to fix the treasure. Carefully replace the other items in your box so they will be ready for your next "take-it-apart session."

EXPLORING

MY OWN EXPLORATIONS

GET SET TO EXPLORE

Get set for exploring by making yourself a portable science kit. Find an old lunch box with a thermos (perferably a workman's type with a wide-mouth thermos), add your science log, sharpened pencils, microscope and binoculars (they don't cost as much as you think), dull-bladed knife, old fork and spoon, plastic or paper cups with tight-fitting tops (save from fast-food restaurants), plastic zip-close bags, rubber bands, paper clips and other odds and ends. The thermos can be used to hold samples of puddle water, tadpoles or underwater plants collected for your aquarium. The lunch box's inside compartments will be just right for separating materials to be taken home or to the classroom for further study or classification for a collection. Not only is it compact and easy to carry, it will keep all your supplies organized and ready to go at a moment's notice. This kit should take you from the woods and streams to the park or city sidewalk and back again with enough gear to earn you the title of "explorer."

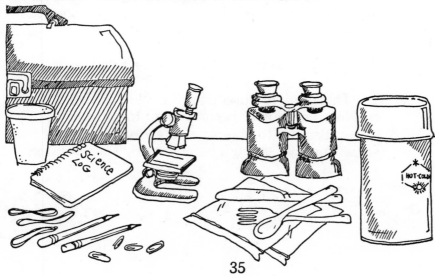

THE COLLECTION CONNECTION

Making, organizing and sharing collections of things of scientific interest is one of the very best ways to learn more about using scientific skills and processes. The true scientist is called on constantly to observe, explore, investigate, experiment, infer, classify and value.

How many of these words do you know the exact meaning of? How many do you think you have had scientific experience with?

One of the best ways to begin feeling and behaving in a scientific manner is to begin your own science collection.

Some suggestions to help you get started are:

1. Think before collecting — decide on *one* thing of real interest to you that you want to learn more about. Be sure to choose a category that makes sense and that you will be able to be successful with.

For example, if you live several hundred miles from the beach, seashells or ocean plant life would probably not be a good collection for you. In the same manner, if you hate getting burs and stickers all over you, and you really don't like hiking in the woods, you would not want to begin a wildflower or leaf collection.

2.   Try to begin a collection that you think will hold your interest for awhile — once you get a good start, you will most likely want to make many collections over the years. But, it is best to concentrate on one at a time and learn all about that one, at least while "scientific collecting" is still new to you.

3.   Organize the tools of your trade — (that's the way the real scientists do it) think about what you will need to hold, experiment with and display your collection. Make a list and begin to gather the necessary supplies and equipment. Then, organize it for use at a moment's notice. Will you need scissors, paper, pails, a log book, hammer and nails, screw-top jars, nets, boxes, or other materials?

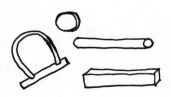

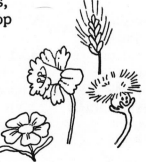

4. Begin to collect resource materials to help you become a scientific expert — books, magazines, kits, and most importantly, people who already know a lot about your subject.

5. Plan how you will preserve and display your collection — this is a most important step because unclassified items thrown randomly into containers or packed into closets will be neither educational nor enjoyable. Make a rule too, not to collect more than you can efficiently display.

Now you are ready to start! What will your first collection be?

- leaves
- flowers
- rocks
- fossils
- shells
- snail shells
- bark
- litter
- fabric

- nuts, bolts or screws
- birds' feathers
- clock and watch works
- magnets
- seedpods
- roots

CATCH 'EM QUICK

To make a nifty bug catcher for excursions and exploration, here's what to do ...

Use a mop or broom handle, a wire coat hanger and an old nylon hose to make a net. Use the net to catch some insects to study. Be sure to catch only non-poisonous ones such as butterflies and grasshoppers (no spiders or wasps). Then, make some temporary homes for your insects. After studying their actions at close range for a time, release them outdoors. Save your bug catcher for another time when you are ready to investigate some other kinds of bugs.

UP, UP AND AWAY

Kitemaking and kiteflying are ancient arts originating in China. Chinese legend tells us that kites were flown before a battle or to ward off evil spirits. Most were made of rice paper and bamboo and were decorated with bird and animal images.

Try making your own kite. There are several different kinds. You may want to make a box kite, a triangle or diamond-shaped kite, a windsock or even a traditional Chinese fish kite. Your kite can be made from tissue paper, butcher paper, newspaper, mylar or a sturdy brown paper bag. Whatever kind of kite you decide to make, you will need only paper, string, a long flexible stick, glue and plenty of patience. Of course, you can buy one at the store, but then you miss half the fun.

40

Be sure to stand with your back to the wind. Gently let the air lift the kite and watch it soar, dance and dive. If the kite dips to the left, run to left; if it should veer to the right, move in that direction. One good hint to remember is to make a long tail for your kite. It will keep it balanced and upright. So, make your kite, wait for a windy day and go fly it!

ON THE GO

Make a list of field trips you can take to find out about "science all around you." Use the Yellow Pages and other resource books to give you ideas and locations of interest. First, list what you want to find out. Then, decide where and when to go, who you want to take with you and how long it will take. Keep a simple record of the trip and what you learn (add this to your science log). Many towns have museums, observatories and galleries to visit — and don't forget the library, fire station, food processing plant or your own backyard and neighborhood.

SEARCH OUT THE MAGNETS

Bet there are more magnets around than you ordinarily think about. Start a search now and make a record of all you find. Some suggestions for starters are:

- magnetic can openers
- magnetic hammers
- magnetic screwdrivers
- magnetic memo boards
- magnetic latches on cabinets and refrigerator doors
- toys

And, how about the huge magnets used in shipyards, auto plants and on construction sites?

After you have completed your search, try to think of a substitute for the magnet used in each item. Example: What could be used in a magnetic toy car instead of the magnet? Could the car still go as far or as fast? How could the memos be attached to the memo board without the magnets? Would the substitute work as well?

43

STAKE OUT A WATCHING ROCK

Select a good-sized (but not too large to be easily moved) rock to "watch and learn" from. Turn the rock over to see how the ground looks and what kind (if any) plant and animal life grows under it. Place a few leaves, some twigs, pebbles, bits of paper and even food such as bread and hard candy under the rock. Check again at regular intervals to see what changes have taken place. Which material has decayed fastest? Why? What happens to the tiny animals living under the rock when it is left out of place for a while?

LOOK FOR STICKS AND STONES AND OLD BONES

Find some to pick up, examine and question. How long have they been where they are now? How did they get there and how will they be moved to another location? (by humans or animals, by wind or water, etc.) What form were they in previously? (part of a large boulder, an animal, a big tree or a small shrub, etc.) Do they serve a useful purpose where they are now located? Should they be moved or left where they are? Would the environment be in a better or worse state without them?

HOLD A PIECE OF THE WORLD IN YOUR HANDS

To begin your expedition, ask permission to borrow a small shovel and to dig up a plot of earth large enough for you to investigate. (Make sure the soil is from a vacant lot or a place where no one will mind if a piece is missing.) Put the earth sample in a pie tin or cardboard box. Use your hands and a magnifying glass to examine all the different things that make up the soil. Do you see grasses, roots, insects, clay, pebbles, leaves or a worm? Make a list of the items you find, and see if you can determine how they depend upon each other.

STUDY A STREAM

Find the nearest creek or stream and spend a little time investigating.

- Observe how fast the water is moving.
- Move some stones around to see how it changes the flow of the water.
- Take an old colander to scoop up water and sediment from a shallow part of the stream. Dump the contents remaining in the colander on a piece of cloth. Sort through them to see what's at the bottom of the stream — shells, soil, pebbles, fossils, maybe small animals and plants. Look at them through your microscope.
- Collect a sample of water in a jar with a screw-on lid to take home to watch. What happens as the sediment settles to the bottom? What does this tell you about the stream?

EXPERIMENTING

MY OWN EXPERIMENTS

IF YOU WERE A SCIENTIST, NAME YOUR EXPERIMENT

Sometimes people forget how hard scientists work to find ways to make the world a cleaner, healthier and more pleasant place to live. We take for granted the long hours of study and hard work that scientists spend to find ways to purify the air we breathe, to find cures for diseases and to preserve and discover new uses for the earth's natural resources. Actually, the research and successful experimentation that is taking place in science laboratories right now is helping people all over the world live longer and better lives.

If you were a well-trained scientist with a laboratory of your own, what research or experiment would you like to be conducting to find a way to make our world a cleaner and healthier place to live?

Write a brief description of the experiment or research and begin to look in magazines, library books or textbooks to see if other scientists are working on your experiment.

LOG IT!

To help you begin to think and act like a real scientist, you need a well organized and "ready to use" science log. It doesn't have to be fancy or complicated — a simple loose-leaf or spiral-bound notebook will do nicely. Make an attractive cover, and set it up with a table of contents, glossary (list of terms and what they mean), things you want to find out, clippings from magazines and newspapers and other "scientific" information. Be sure to record your investigations, explorations and the results of your experiments. Remember, it's *your* science log. Make it work for you!

MAKE YOUR OWN WEATHER STATION

By conducting the following experiments, you will gain a little insight into the world of weather.

Why does it rain?

Partially fill a saucepan with water. Let it come to a boil. Hold the pan lid over the pan, but not on it. First, you will see a thin layer of steam covering the lid. Then, as the water continues to boil, tiny drops of water form on the lid and fall back into the pan.

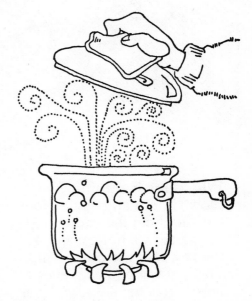

When water is heated, it evaporates and turns into steam. When cooled, it condenses and becomes water again. This is why it rains. Droplets of water form a cloud, and when the drops are cooled and get too heavy, they fall to the ground as rain.

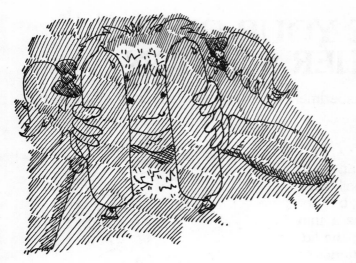

Why does it lightning?

Blow up two long balloons and go stand in a dark room or closet. Rub the balloons on your clothing, a rug or the curtains. Hold each end of the balloon, one to the other, almost touching. If the room is dark enough, there will be a spark of electricity between the two balloons. This results from friction. If the same thing happens between two clouds, the result is lightning.

Why does it thunder?

Blow air into an empty paper bag and hold the end tightly so the air will not escape. Hit the bag with the other hand. The bag will pop with a loud noise. This happens when air rushes together. Lightning in the sky forces air apart, so when the air rushes together again, it thunders.

SOCK-IT-TO-THE-SOIL

Most likely, you have planted something and waited for it to grow — seeds, bulbs or cuttings from other plants. Bet you never thought about planting your sock.

The best time to carry out this project is on a sunny day in late summer or early fall. Find an old, fuzzy worn-out sock that will fit *over* one of your shoes. Wander over to a nearby lot full of weeds and grass and walk back and forth through the underbrush. Then, take the sock off and examine the kinds of seeds that are stuck to the sock. Put some potting soil into a medium-sized baking pan and plant the sock! Cover it with a thin layer of soil and water thoroughly. Watch to see what happens within a week or so — some of the seeds should begin to sprout! Even if your sock garden fails to flourish, you will have had a fine time stalking seeds and carrying out this scientific experiment.

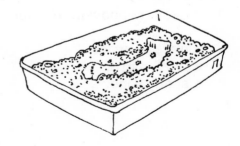

AFTER A STORM . . .

You don't have to search for rainbows! You can make your own. Remember, rainbows are created when sunlight hits raindrops or water which separates all the colors in the sun. Can you name the seven rainbow colors?

To make a rainbow *inside*, you will need:

- a glass of water
- a small mirror
- a sunny window

... A RAINBOW OF COURSE

1. Place the mirror in the glass of water.
2. Place the glass so the sun can shine on the mirror.
3. Turn the glass until a rainbow is reflected against the wall or ceiling.

Now that you have become a rainbow-maker, you should be sure to keep looking for the ones that follow real rains — they are truly scientific marvels to behold.

AIR FARE

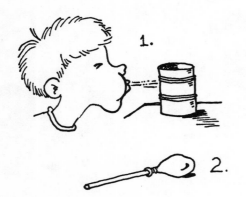

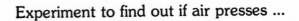

Experiment to find out if air presses ...

Stand a tin can on a table and try to blow it over. Fasten a balloon to the end of a straw. Lay the balloon on the table and stand the tin can on it. Now, blow into the straw.

Stand a large book on a table and try to blow it over. Take a paper bag, make a neck in it and stand the book on the bag. Blow into the neck of the bag.

Experiment to find out if air contains water ...

Fill a large, completely dry glass jar with ice. Observe as the jar becomes wet on the outside. Can you tell why the air around the jar was cooled *outside* by the ice *inside* the jar?

COLOR RAMA

Make your own color rama to show how all the magnificent colors we see around us are made from only three primary colors: red, yellow and blue.

1.   Spread a large sheet of paper (the larger the better) on the table or floor.
2.   Peel the paper off the fattest primary color crayons in your box (or use colored chalk).
3.   Begin to make large sweeps with one color, using the sides of the crayon.
4.   Continue making the sweeps until red crosses blue to form violet; yellow crosses blue to form green; red crosses yellow to form orange, etc.

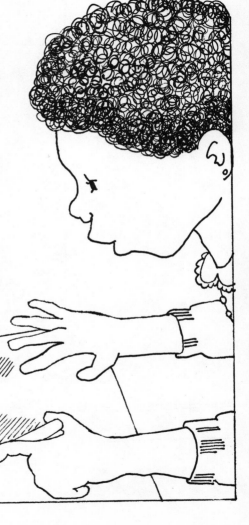

JACK-OF-ALL-LIGHTS

You may want to save this experiment with fire and air for Halloween week, or you may just want to use it as a scientific experiment anytime you have a pumpkin, a knife, a candle, some sand and water and the time to do some experimenting.

First, cut the top off the pumpkin just as you would to make a jack-'o-lantern (but don't cut a face yet). Next, put a candle in the pumpkin and light it with a match. Let it begin to burn. Then, put the top back on the pumpkin.

What happened? Why did the candle flame go out? Find out more about why fire can not burn without air.

Put the candle on a saucer and light it again. Place a glass over the candle and watch what happens when the flame gets no oxygen.

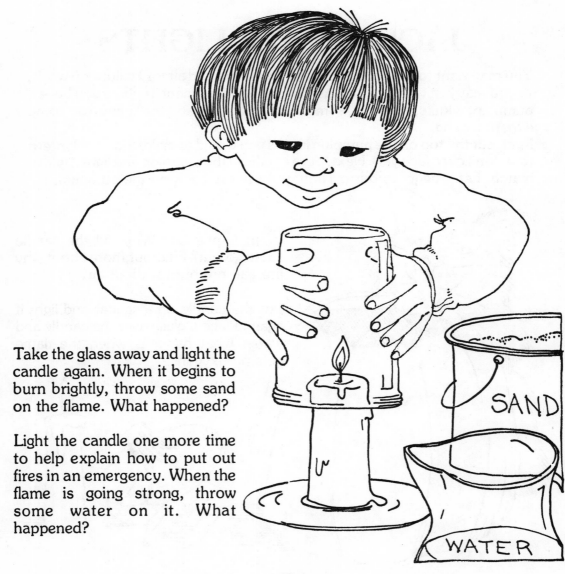

Take the glass away and light the candle again. When it begins to burn brightly, throw some sand on the flame. What happened?

Light the candle one more time to help explain how to put out fires in an emergency. When the flame is going strong, throw some water on it. What happened?

SAND

WATER

Now, back to jolly old Jack-Of-All-Lights.

Cut out the funniest face you can think of — eyes, nose, mouth, teeth — use your imagination to make him merry and bright. Now, put the candle back inside, light it and put the top on. Even with the top on, your candle will continue to give off a golden glow for several hours. Why did giving Jack a jolly face keep the flame from going out?

CHANGEABLE JACK

Your Halloween jack-'o-lantern has much more to offer after the big holiday has passed. If you haven't already done so, light a candle and let it burn inside the jack-'o-lantern for an hour or so. Blow the candle out and remove. Now Jack will slowly take on a new form. Place him outside in a place where you can easily go and have a look from time to time during the next few weeks. Note the changes occurring in the pumpkin. Has mold begun to grow? Is his face getting wrinkled and starting to sag? The decaying process has begun. This is the same thing that happens to food that is left on the ground. The mold helps break the food down so it becomes a part of the soil and then provides food for other plants. You have now helped the balance of nature to continue by experimenting with a "Changeable Jack."

SPORE YOU KNOW IT

Not all plants grow from seeds. Some grow from spores. To see some spores firsthand, try this experiment.

Leave a piece of bread out overnight to expose it to the air. Then, put the bread in a large jar. Close the jar tightly. Make sure the bread is kept moist. In a few days, a bluish-gray mold will appear. Then it will turn green. When this occurs, take the bread out of the jar and turn it upside down while gently tapping it. The spores will fall off.

HIGH-RISE BREAD BAKE

Did you know that yeast is a spore too? Yeast plants grow with warmth, moisture and just a little sugar (too much sugar slows down the growth). As the tiny plants grow, they produce gas bubbles called carbon dioxide. As the bubbles spread throughout a flour, oil and liquid mixture, the dough becomes light and porous and begins to rise.

As bread bakes, the yeast is killed by the heat. The liquid in the bread then becomes steam and raises the bread.

Use this super-simple recipe to bake High-Rise Bread so you can observe firsthand, the scientific process that takes place in bread baking. Bet you will never take for granted another slice of bread as just "ordinary food."

½ yeast cake
1 cup warm water
½ tablespoon sugar

½ teaspoon salt
2 cups flour
½ stick butter

Dissolve the yeast cake in warm water. Stir in remaining ingredients. Pour into greased bowl and let rise until dough doubles, about 1½ - 2 hours. Punch dough down and put in greased 9-inch pie pan. Let rise until double. Melt butter and pour over dough before baking. Bake at 400° for approximately 45 minutes.

Serve big slices of your High-Rise Bread with fresh butter and honey. As you eat, discuss the manner in which the yeast bread was formed and the scientific processes involved in the marvel of 100% pure honey-bee honey and in making butter.

EVAPORATION IN ACTION

Evaporation is happening around you all the time. Can you think of an example of evaporation? Try these simple experiments to see evaporation in action.

Fill a glass almost full of water. Mark the water level with a rubber band or piece of colored cellophane tape. Place the glass in a window and check it each day to see what is happening. Where does the water go?

Drop some water on two identical squares of construction paper. Place the squares side by side on a table. Fan one of the dampened squares with a piece of paper or cardboard. Why does moving air hasten evaporation?

Go outside right after a rainstorm to find a puddle to watch.
Check every day to see what is happening.
Keep a record of how fast the water disappears.
Where did the water go?

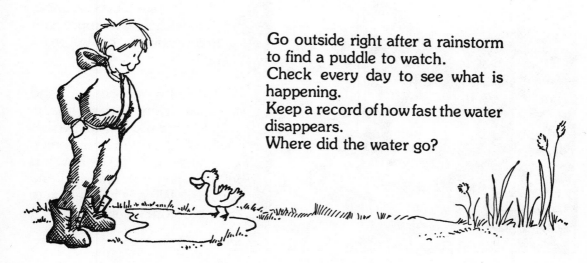

FROM A BALL OF ROOTS TO NEW GREEN SHOOTS

An old, dried up bulb is not much to look at. Usually, it is brown and shriveled and looks like something you would throw out with the kitchen garbage.

If you take a second look however, and this time view a bulb with the eyes of a scientist, what you see is much more exciting. Actually, the bulb, which at first glance looks like a ball of old roots covered with tiny dried up leaves, is really an underground bud covered with bud scales. It is all ready to be planted in soil to demonstrate the miracle of new growth. Onions, tulips, daffodils, lilies and garlic are just a few of the beautiful and productive plants that grow from a dried up old bulb. Can you name one other plant that comes from a bulb?

Here is a simple experiment that will help you appreciate how plants grow from bulbs.

1. Take an onion and place it in a dark, warm place for a week or two.
2. Check on the onion occasionally to see how it is changing in looks, feel and smell. What is happening to the onion?

3. Fill a small pot with soil and bury the onion bulb in the soil. Place the pot in a light and airy spot, give it a good drink of water every day or so and see what happens.

4. How many days will it be before you see the new green shoots that tell you that your tired old bulb is alive and well again?

5. Keep a record of the time it takes for the onion bulb to grow into a new plant.

By conducting this simple experiment you will see firsthand how new plants grow from bulbs.

BALLOON POWER

1. Blow up a balloon and tie a knot at the open end. Hold the balloon over your head and let it go. What happens?

2. Blow up a balloon. Hold the end together with your fingers. Hold it over your head and let it go. What happens?

3. Which way does the balloon go? In which direction does the air go? Follow the directions again in #2, but instead of holding the full balloon over your head, hold it out in front of you and let it go. What happens?

4. Blow up your balloon. Tie the open end and place it on water. What happens? (If you don't have a puddle or stream, a tub filled with water works great!)

5. Place a blown-up balloon (open end *not* tied) on water. Let go of the open end and watch it go! What happens if the open end goes under the water?

THE RACE IS ON

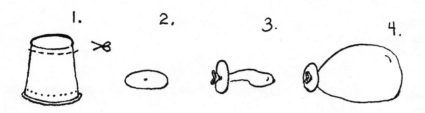

Cut the bottoms off two paper cups. Make holes in the center of each bottom piece. Pull the open end of a balloon through each hole. Blow up the balloons. Hold your fingers around the openings and place them on the water. Let go and see which balloon goes the fastest! This could also be fun to do with a friend.

HOW DOES YOUR GARDEN GROW?

To make a chemical garden, you will need these things:

- glass pie plate
- porous rocks
- charcoal briquets
- sponge pieces
- jar
- 6 tablespoons salt
- 6 tablespoons laundry bluing
- 3 tablespoons household ammonia
- food coloring
- twigs
- acorns

Sprinkle the rocks, charcoal and sponge pieces with water. Arrange these in the pie plate. Mix the chemicals in the jar using only 3 tablespoons of the salt. Pour the mixture in the pie plate, dampening all the items thoroughly. Drop a little food coloring on the top of the arrangement. Sprinkle the remaining 3 tablespoons of salt over the creation. Add twigs, acorns or other odds and ends to give it more of a garden feel.

In a few hours, crystals will begin to form on the materials. Add more of the chemical mixture if some places seem bare. Watch the crystal growth for several days. What do you think caused the crystals to grow? Find out how this type of growth occurs.

MAGNET MAGIC

Use magnets to discover ...
- What objects magnet attract.
  Put several different objects in a box (nails, chalk, tacks, crayons, paper clips, pennies, pencils, etc.). Tie a magnet onto a string. Lower the magnet into the box to see which items the magnet attracts.

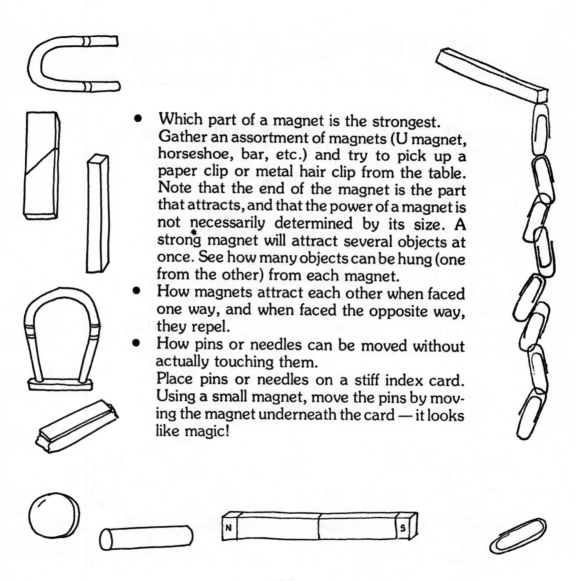

- Which part of a magnet is the strongest.
  Gather an assortment of magnets (U magnet, horseshoe, bar, etc.) and try to pick up a paper clip or metal hair clip from the table. Note that the end of the magnet is the part that attracts, and that the power of a magnet is not necessarily determined by its size. A strong magnet will attract several objects at once. See how many objects can be hung (one from the other) from each magnet.
- How magnets attract each other when faced one way, and when faced the opposite way, they repel.
- How pins or needles can be moved without actually touching them.
  Place pins or needles on a stiff index card. Using a small magnet, move the pins by moving the magnet underneath the card — it looks like magic!

MORE MAGNET MAGIC

Did you ever dream of being in total control of a sailboat? Here's your chance!

You will need:
- a flat piece of light wood or bark
- a nail
- cardboard
- scissors
- plastic drinking straw
- glue
- large flat pan
- water
- magnet

This is what you do:
1. Cut out a sail from the cardboard.
2. Run the drinking straw through the sail.
3. Glue the straw to the wood or bark to make a "sailboat."
4. Fill the pan almost full of water.
5. Place the boat in the water and lay the nail on the wood.
6. Use the magnet to draw the boat to you. Move around the pan to make the boat "sail" in different directions.

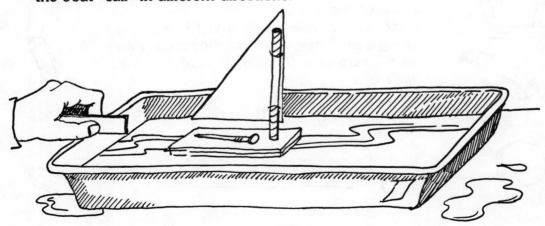

LEMON-UP FOR LEMONADE

Have you ever taken a scientific look at a lemon? Take a lemon in both hands and feel it. How does the skin feel? How does the lemon smell? Now, cut the lemon in half. Does it smell different? Squeeze a little juice on your finger and taste it — is it sweet or bitter? Are there seeds inside? Save a few to plant — you may be lucky enough to grow your own lemon tree. By the way, do you know how lemon trees look, and what kind of climate they grow in? People sometimes sprinkle lemon juice on other fruits to keep them from turning brown when sliced for salads. Can you find out why lemon juice is better for this purpose than other fruit juices?